Discover Bugs

by Amanda Trane

© 2017 by Amanda Trane
ISBN: 978-1-53240-2555
eISBN: 978-1-53240-2562
Images licensed from Fotolia.com
All rights reserved.
No portion of this book may be reproduced
without express permission of the publisher.
First Edition
Published in the United States by
Xist Publishing
www.xistpublishing.com
PO Box 61593 Irvine, CA 92602

2

There are many different kinds of insects. All bugs are insects, but not all insects are bugs. Some creatures we call bugs, are not even insects! All insects have six legs when they grow up.

It can be difficult to count the legs of any creature. This is a tarantula spider. It has eight legs, so it is not an insect.

5

This scorpion has eight legs, so it is not an insect. Scorpions eat insects.

This is a webworm moth. It has six legs, with three legs on each side.

Legs are not the only thing we have to remember. Caterpillars are insects, even though they have more than six legs. When it is an adult, it will have six legs.

This Morpho Butterfly was once a caterpillar. Now it has six small legs.

13

14

This dragonfly has a very small head, a short thorax, and a long abdomen.

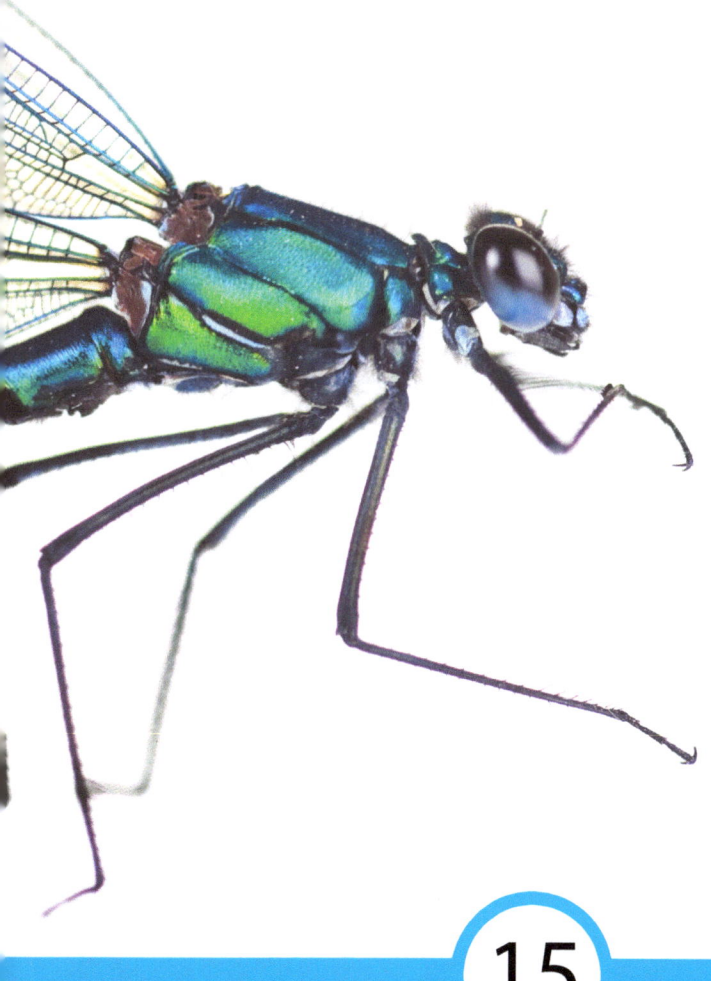

If you are not sure where the thorax ends and the abdomen begins, look for the legs. The back legs on this green locust show where the thorax ends.

18

This is a House fly. Some people kill house flies with bug spray, but they are not true bugs, they are insects.

Ants are insects, but they are not bugs! True bugs have a mouth like a straw, but ants have mouths like scissors that open and shut.

Bees help fruit and flowers grow. Some people are afraid of bee stings, and think they are bad bugs. They are not bugs! They are important insects, but they have a different mouth than true bugs.

This is a Stick bug. It is not a true bug! It eats leaves from trees and does not have a mouth like a straw.

This Ladybug is not a true bug either! It has a strong mouth that it uses to eat tiny bugs called aphids.

This is a leaf bug or Katydid. It is not a true bug either! It hides in the leaves that it eats.

This is a praying mantis. A praying mantis has six legs and shows the three parts of an insect. It has a small head, a long thorax, and a big abdomen.

This is a Scentless Plant bug. It is the only true bug in this book. True bugs look almost exactly the same as babies as they do when they are adults.

www.ingramcontent.com/pod-product-compliance
Lightning Source LLC
LaVergne TN
LVHW010020070426
835507LV00001B/17